SUCCEEDING IN SCIENCE
SCIENCE & TECHNOLOGY SERIES
A Set of 7 Books for Years 1 to 7
Book 2   -   (Year 2)

GW00633417

CONTENTS

CHAPTER 1 - ON THE MOVE

'Transport' is the word we use when we talk about the **way** people and goods **move** from **place** to **place**.

People did not always have the same means of transport (moving about) as we have today.

Below we have drawn **6 early** types of transport.

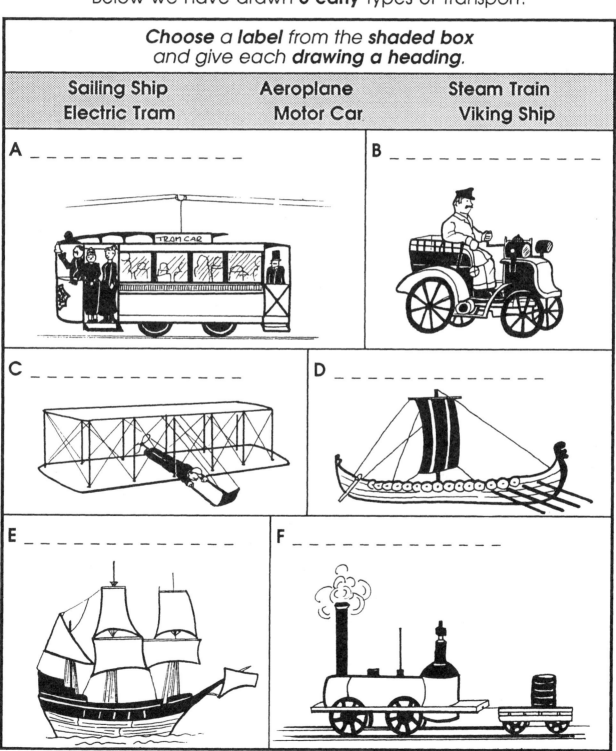

Choose a label from the shaded box and give each drawing a heading.

| Sailing Ship | Aeroplane | Steam Train |
| Electric Tram | Motor Car | Viking Ship |

A _ _ _ _ _ _ _ _ _ _ _

B _ _ _ _ _ _ _ _ _ _ _

C _ _ _ _ _ _ _ _ _ _ _

D _ _ _ _ _ _ _ _ _ _ _

E _ _ _ _ _ _ _ _ _ _ _

F _ _ _ _ _ _ _ _ _ _ _

1 - ON THE MOVE

Here are some **modern** means of **transport** that are used
to **move** people from **place** to **place.**

*Transport can take us by **land, water, air** or **space**.*
We have drawn some of each for you to colour in.
*Use **green** for **land** transport,*
***blue** for **water** transport,*
***yellow** for **air** transport,*
***red** for **space** transport.*

1 - ON THE MOVE

**What can you tell from the drawings
that you just coloured in on page 4 ?**

*For exercises **1** to **5,** put a **tick beside**
the **right** set of words to **finish** each of the sentences.*

1 **To get by road from Sydney to Melbourne**
(a) you would drive a car. ____
(b) you would catch a plane. ____

2 **If you wanted to sail on the water**
(a) you would use a motor boat. ____
(b) you would use a sailing boat. ____

3 **The faster form of air travel would be**
(a) by helicopter. ____
(b) by aeroplane. ____

4 **A ocean liner is used to carry passengers**
(a) over water. ____
(b) through the air. ____

5 **A rocket is used to travel**
(a) to another country. ____
(b) into space. ____

*For exercises **6** to **10**, **write** either **'yes'** or **'no'**
to the following questions.*

6 Would it be quicker to travel by ship
than by plane ? _____

7 Would a bus carry more passengers
than a train ? _____

8 Would it be possible to walk around
on an ocean liner ? _____

9 It is possible to drive from Sydney
to Canberra ? _____

10 Is it possible to sail from Sydney
to Hobart ? _____

1 - ON THE MOVE

As well as getting people from place to place,
transport is also used to get **goods** (like food and petrol)
and **services** (like mail) **from place to place**.

Below we have **7** forms of **transport** that carry **goods or services**.
Choose a **word** from the **shaded box** to label each drawing
with the **goods** or **service** that it **transports**.

Mail   Soil   Cars   Food   Petrol   Papers   Cement

A _ _ _ _ _ _ _ _

B _ _ _ _ _ _ _

C _ _ _ _ _ _ _

D _ _ _ _ _ _ _

E _ _ _ _ _ _ _

F _ _ _ _ _ _ _

G _ _ _ _ _ _ _

1 - ON THE MOVE

**What can you tell from the drawings
that you just coloured in on page 6 ?**

*For exercises 1 to 6, put a tick beside
the right set of words to finish each of the sentences.*

1   The man on the motor bike is delivering
(a) mail.   _____
(b) petrol.   _____

2   The tip truck is carrying
(a) food.   _____
(b) garden soil.   _____

3   The oil tanker is transporting
(a) cement.   _____
(b) petrol.   _____

4   The Pete's Poultry truck is carrying
(a) food.   _____
(b) bird cages.   _____

5   The cement is being carried
(a) in an oil tanker.   _____
(b) by a mixer truck.   _____

6   The cars are being transported
(a) by rail.   _____
(b) by road.   _____

*For exercises 7 to 9, write either 'yes' or 'no'
to the following questions.*

7   Could garden soil be transported by
a cement truck ?   _ _ _ _ _

8   Do you think that Pete's Poultry
truck would need to be cold inside ?   _ _ _ _ _

9   Do you think the four cars on the
special delivery trailer are new ?   _ _ _ _ _

1 - ON THE MOVE

Emergency transport.
In **emergencies**, such as accidents and fires for example,
special **vehicles** (*forms of transport*) can be used.

Choose a **heading** from the **shaded box** below
to **label** each of the drawings **of emergency transport**.

Ambulance	Surf Rescue	Police Car	Fire Engine
Flying Doctor		Rescue Helicopter	

A _ _ _ _ _ _ _ _ _ _ _ _ _ _

B _ _ _ _ _ _ _ _ _ _ _ _ _

C _ _ _ _ _ _ _ _ _ _ _ _ _ _

D _ _ _ _ _ _ _ _ _ _ _ _ _

E _ _ _ _ _ _ _ _ _ _

F _ _ _ _ _ _ _ _ _ _ _

1 - ON THE MOVE

What can you tell from the drawings that you just coloured in on page 8 ?

*For exercises 1 to 5, put a **tick beside** the **right** set of words to **finish** each of the sentences.*

1   A fire engine, using its siren, could
(a) be on its way to a bushfire.   ____
(b) be on its way to a surfing accident.   ____

2   A rescue helicopter would be used
(a) to rescue people from a sinking boat.   ____
(b) to take pictures of a boat race.   ____

3   A police car is always called
(a) to an accident on the water.   ____
(b) to a serious road accident.   ____

4   The flying doctor is called to sick people
(a) in the outback areas of Australia.   ____
(b) in cities .   ____

5   An ambulance is often carrying
(a) visitors to hospital.   ____
(b) sick people to hospital.   ____

*For exercises 6 to 10, **write** either **'yes'** or **'no'** to the following questions.*

6   Could a surf rescue boat be
used to help a swimmer in trouble ?   _____

7   Would a fire engine be of help in
a house fire ?   _____

8   Would the flying doctor take you
from home to school ?   _____

9   Would a police car carry policemen
to the scene of a robbery ?   _____

10   Are ambulances often called to
road accidents ?   _____

1 - ON THE MOVE

Nothing that **carries** people or goods about can **move** by
itself.   Some form of **power** is needed to
move every type of transport.

Wind power blows sailing boats and wind surfers along.
Engine power is needed to move cars and aeroplanes.
People power is what moves a rowing boat through the water.

Colour each drawing below.
*Use **purple** for things using **wind** power.*
*Use **red** for things using **engine** power.*
*Use **orange** for things using **people** power.*

1 - ON THE MOVE

What can you tell from the drawings that you just coloured in on page 10 ?

*Put a **tick beside** the **right** set of words to **finish** each sentence.*

1   **The sailing boat and the wind surfer are being**
   (a) blown along by the wind.   ____
   (b) pulled along by a motor.   ____

2   **The rowing boat is being pulled**
   (a) through the water by rowers.   ____
   (b) through the water by a rower.   ____

3   **The glider and the hot air balloon**
   (a) are being moved by the wind.   ____
   (b) are being driven by engines.   ____

4   **To fly through the air, the aeroplane**
   (a) needs an engine and a pilot.   ____
   (b) needs sails and a good wind.   ____

5   **The surf rescue boat moves through the water**
   (a) by being rowed by the lifesavers.   ____
   (b) using its outboard motor.   ____

6   **The bicycle needs a**
   (a) motor to move it.   ____
   (b) person to pedal it.   ____

7   **The roller blade rider uses the power**
   (a) of the wind.   ____
   (b) of his legs.   ____

8   **The bus and the train both**
   (a) run on the road.   ____
   (b) need an engine and a driver.   ____

1 - ON THE MOVE

We need to **make sure** when we move from place to place that we are **as safe as possible.**

The top row of drawings show **4 safety measures** (**A**, **B**, **C** and **D**).

Below are drawn **4 examples** of **places** *where these safety measures should be used.*

*Use **green** to colour **A** and the **place where it should be used.***
*Use **yellow** to colour **B** and the **place where it should be used.***
*Use **blue** to colour **C** and the **place where it should be used.***
*Use **red** to colour **D** and the **place where it should be used.***

1 - ON THE MOVE

What can you tell from the drawings that you just coloured in on page 12 ?

*Put a **tick beside** the **right** set of words to **finish** each sentence.*

1 **The drawing in Box A**
   (a) shows a life-jacket. ____
   (b) shows a winter jacket. ____

2 **The drawing in Box B**
   (a) shows a space helmet. ____
   (b) shows a safety helmet. ____

3 **The drawing in Box C**
   (a) shows a policeman. ____
   (b) shows a 'lollipop' man. ____

4 **The drawing in Box D**
   (a) shows a lounge chair. ____
   (b) shows a car seat-belt. ____

5 **A person riding a motor bike**
   (a) must wear a life-jacket. ____
   (b) must wear a safety helmet. ____

6 **Seat-belts have to be worn by**
   (a) people riding in cars. ____
   (b) people sailing in boats. ____

7 **A 'lollipop' person helps**
   (a) children at school crossings. ____
   (b) serves in the school tuckshop. ____

8 **A person sailing in a boat**
   (a) must wear a seat-belt. ____
   (b) must wear a life-jacket. ____

1 - ON THE MOVE

Here is a **transport findaword** to finish off this topic.

```
          S E A
        B A L L O O N
      T R A I N     S K Y
      S A I L O R     B U S
      D R I V E R       R O W
      R O A D           R A I L
    W H E E L S   C A N O E   F E R R Y
    L I N E R   L A U N C H   S P A C E
  W I N G S     W H A R F   B I K E   C A R
  G L I D E R   R O C K E T     P L A N E
  S A I L S   O C E A N   T R U C K   T U G
  P I L O T   F L Y E R   R U N W A Y
  S T A T I O N   T A X I   A I R P O R T
```

There are **33** words to be found in the findaword.
They are all to do with **one** of the three forms of **transport**.
This will give you **11 words** for each of the **3 headings** below.

As you find each word, write it under its correct heading.

Land transport	Water transport	Air transport

CHAPTER 2 - OUR WEATHER

Weather is the word we use when we talk about
rain, temperature and **wind.**

Weather also **includes** things like
snow, hail, clouds, sunshine and storms.

Weather affects lots of things,
what we wear, what we eat and the types of houses we live in.

Here we have drawn pictures showing **6** different
types of weather.
Label the **pictures** using a **heading** from the **shaded box.**

Cloudy	Cold	Sunny	Wet	Windy	Hot

A _ _ _ _ _ _ _ _

B _ _ _ _ _ _ _ _

C _ _ _ _ _ _ _ _

D _ _ _ _ _ _ _ _

E _ _ _ _ _ _ _ _

F _ _ _ _ _ _ _ _

2 - OUR WEATHER

How is rain formed ?

Water from oceans, rivers and lakes provides most of the **water** that becomes **rain**.

Plants also give off a certain amount of **water**.

Here we have diagrams explaining how water becomes rain.
This is called the **Water Cycle**.
*1 - (a) Use **blue** to colour the diagram showing **rain falling**.*
*(b) Use **green** to colour the diagram showing **water rising**.*

The heat from the sun causes water to rise up from oceans, rivers, lakes and plants.

The cool air in the sky collects the water into clouds and sometimes rain falls.

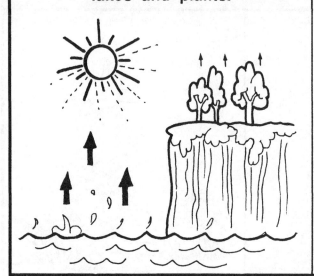 

Water that forms into clouds **mainly** falls as **rain**.
But at times it can come back to the earth as **fog, hail** or **snow**.
*2 - Choose a **word** from the **shaded box** to label each drawing.*

Rain	Fog	Hail	Snow

A _ _ _ _ _ _

B _ _ _ _ _ _

C _ _ _ _ _ _

D _ _ _ _ _ _

2 - OUR WEATHER

What can you tell from the diagram and drawings on page 16 ?

*For exercises 1 to 5, put a **tick beside** the **right** set of words to **finish** each of the sentences.*

1 **The heat from the sun causes**
   (a) water to fall from rivers.   ____
   (b) water to rise from rivers.   ____

2 **The cool air in the sky**
   (a) collects water into clouds.   ____
   (b) collects the sunshine.   ____

3 **Plants also give off some**
   (a) water into the air.   ____
   (b) perfume into the clouds.   ____

4 **More rain would fall in places that are**
   (a) near oceans and rivers.   ____
   (b) a long way from oceans and rivers.   ____

5 **Forests with lots of trees would be**
   (a) more likely to have lots of rain.   ____
   (b) unlikely to have lots of rain.   ____

*For exercises 6 to 10, **write** either **'yes'** or **'no'** to the following questions.*

6 Do you think it would be wise to stay out in a heavy hail storm ?   _____

7 Could you build a snowman out of fog ?   _____

8 Would you be colder out in the snow than out in the rain ?   _____

9 Do you think it would be hard driving a car in fog ?   _____

10 Do you think much water would rise from rivers and oceans at night ?   _____

2 - OUR WEATHER

What is temperature ?

Temperature is the amount of **heat** in the **air**.

Temperature can be **measured** with the help of a **thermometer**.
A thermometer measures from
0°C (freezing point) to **100°C** (boiling point).

---

*Below we have **4 pictures** of days with **4 different temperatures**.
Beside each picture is a **thermometer**.*
Can you fill in each thermometer with the day's temperature ?

DAY A
Warm with a temperature of **30°C**

°C
100
90
80
70
60
50
40
30
20
10
0

DAY B
Hot with a temperature **40°C**

°C
100
90
80
70
60
50
40
30
20
10
0

DAY C
Cool with a temperature **20°C**

°C
100
90
80
70
60
50
40
30
20
10
0

DAY D
Cold with a temperature of **10°C**

°C
100
90
80
70
60
50
40
30
20
10
0

2 - OUR WEATHER

**What can you tell from the pictures and the
temperatures that you just filled in on page 18 ?**

*For exercises 1 to 5, put a tick beside
the right set of words to finish each of the sentences.*

1   The girl is at the beach on
(a) the hottest day.   ____
(b) a warm day.   ____

2   On the coldest day
(a) the boy is wearing a jumper.   ____
(b) grandpa is wrapped up in a scarf.   ____

3   The girl has picked some flowers
(a) on the cool day.   ____
(b) on the warm day.   ____

4   On the cool day
(a) the boy is wearing long pants.   ____
(b) the girl is wearing short sleeves.   ____

5   On the day with the temperature at 20°C
(a) grandpa is shivering.   ____
(b) the boy has put on a jumper.   ____

*For exercises 6 to 10, write the correct picture letter
in answer to the following questions.*

6   Which picture shows the coldest day ?   ____

7   Which picture shows the hottest day ?   ____

8   Which day is in between 10°C and 30°C ?   ____

9   Which day is in between 20°C and 40°C ?   ____

10   Which day is a little warmer than Day C ?   ____

2 - OUR WEATHER

What causes wind ?

Wind is the **movement** of **air**.
The thing that causes air to **move** is the **heat** from the **sun**.
When **air heats** up it **rises** and cooler air takes its place.

Winds can blow in many **different strengths**,
and they are graded from **0** (**calm**) to **12** (**hurricane**).

Read the information in the **shaded boxes**.
Write the correct **Grade** of wind above each **drawing**.

Grade 2 Light breeze (tree leaves move gently)	Grade 6 Strong wind (umbrellas misbehave)	Grade 8 Gale (tree branches break)	Grade 10 Storm (trees blow over)	Grade 12 Hurricane (major damage to buildings)

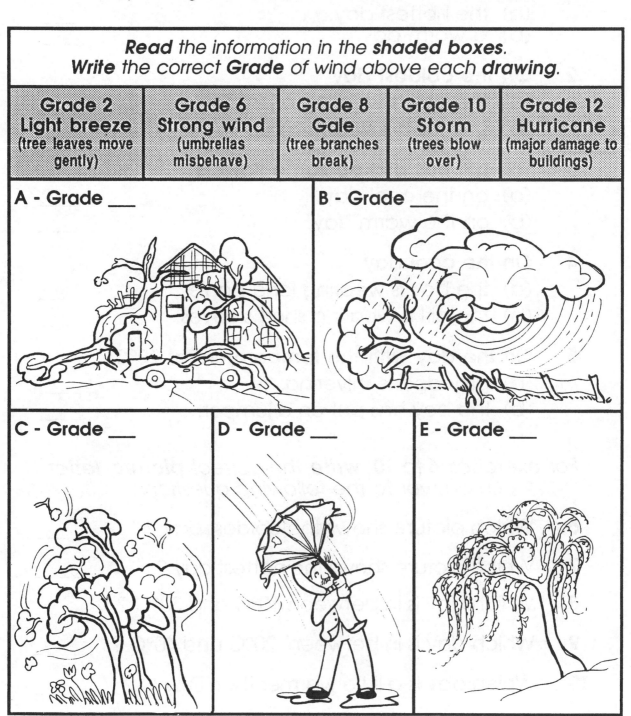

A - Grade ___

B - Grade ___

C - Grade ___

D - Grade ___

E - Grade ___

2 - OUR WEATHER

**What can you tell from the pictures
that you just labelled in on page 20 ?**
*Put a **tick beside** the **right** set of words
to **finish** each sentence.*

1   **The drawings show winds starting with the**
     (a) strongest and ending with the weakest. ____
     (b) weakest and ending with the strongest. ____

2   **A grade 12 wind is called**
     (a) a light breeze.   ____
     (b) a hurricane.   ____

3   **A strong wind**
     (a) is a grade 8 wind.   ____
     (b) is a grade 6 wind.   ____

4   **A grade 10 wind**
     (a) is stronger than a gale.   ____
     (b) is stronger than a hurricane.   ____

5   **A light breeze is a**
     (a) grade 2 wind.   ____
     (b) grade 0 wind.   ____

6   **A gale is**
     (a) stronger than a storm.   ____
     (b) weaker than a storm.   ____

7   **The hurricane has blown**
     (a) the umbrella inside out.   ____
     (b) trees onto the house and the car.   ____

8   **The light breeze is**
     (a) bringing rain.   ____
     (b) gently blowing the willow tree.   ____

2 - OUR WEATHER

The Seasons

Weather is divided **into 4 seasons** and as the **arrows** on the drawings show, they form a **cycle** (each one leading into the next).

In Australia the seasons are as follows.

Spring - *September, October, November*.
Trees and bushes grow new green leaves, spring flowers bloom.
The weather begins to be a little warmer, but this is often quite a windy season.

Summer - *December, January, February.*
Long hot days, lots of sunshine, not much rain. Good beach days but we need to wear protection from the sun. This is also the time of bushfires.

Autumn - *March, April, May.*
Days are cooler, leaves on some trees turn bright red and orange.
This is good picnic weather, but later in the day it can turn cold.

Winter - *June , July, August.*
Days are shorter and quite cold. Some trees have lost all their leaves.
Weather can be wet and windy and on our highest mountains it can snow.

Read all the information above, then label each picture with the correct season.

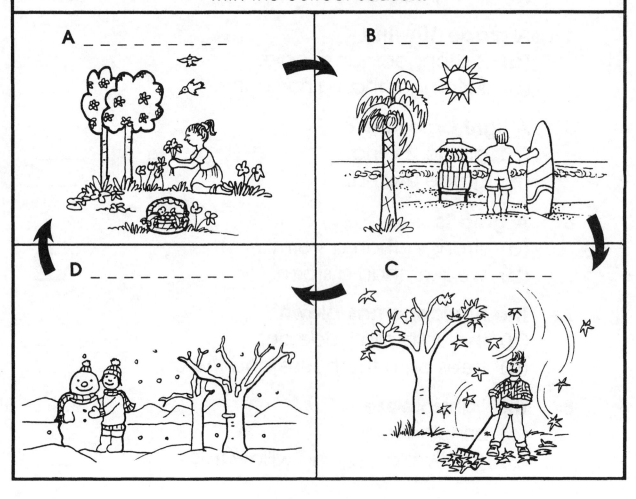

A _ _ _ _ _ _ _ _ _

B _ _ _ _ _ _ _ _ _

D _ _ _ _ _ _ _ _ _

C _ _ _ _ _ _ _ _ _

2 - OUR WEATHER

What can you tell from the information and the pictures that you just labelled on page 22 ?

*For exercises 1 to 6, put a **tick beside** the **right** set of words to **finish** each of the sentences.*

1 **Some trees have no leaves in**
   (a) Winter. ——
   (b) Spring. ——

2 **Winter is**
   (a) colder than Summer. ——
   (b) warmer than Summer. ——

3 **In Summer**
   (a) the days are long and hot. ——
   (b) the days are cold and windy. ——

4 **We are more likely to find snow**
   (a) in the mountains in Summer. ——
   (b) in the mountains in Winter. ——

5 **New leaves appear on trees**
   (a) in Spring. ——
   (b) in Autumn. ——

6 **You would wear warmer clothes**
   (a) in Winter. ——
   (b) in Summer. ——

*Look at the **arrows** on the drawings on **page 22**, then answer questions 7 to 10 with the **name** of a **season**.*

7 Which season follows Spring ? _____

8 Which season follows Autumn ? _____

9 Which season comes before Winter ? _____

10 Which season comes before Summer ? _____

2 - OUR WEATHER

Here is a **WORD PUZZLE** to see
how much you have learned about this topic.

1						O					
2						U					
3						R					
4						W					
5						E					
6						A					
7						T					
8						H					
9						E					
10						R					

Fill in the missing words using the clues below.

1. This word tells us about the temperature on a winter's day.
2. The name of the season that begins in December.
3. The name of the season that ends in November.
4. A word that tells us that there is a lot of air blowing about.
5. The name of the season that begins in June.
6. The name of the thing that brings wet weather.
7. The name of the season that ends in May.
8. The word that tells us that there are very high temperatures.
9. The name of the month that starts Spring.
10. The name of a Grade 10 wind.

CHAPTER 3 - SENDING A MESSAGE

Messages or **information**
can be passed along in many ways.

By **writing** (such as newspapers, magazines and books).
By **talking** (by phone, or radio or television).
By **signs** (such as road signs or warning signs).
By **faces** (the expressions on faces often give a very clear message).

Here we have drawn pictures showing different
ways of sending messages or information.

*Use **blue** to show information given in **writing**.*
*Use **yellow** to show **spoken** messages.*
*Use **red** to colour information given by **signs**.*
*Use **green** to colour messages shown on **faces**.*

3 - SENDING A MESSAGE

Warning Signs

A **sign** is a very **simple** way to get a **message** across.
Most people can **understand** the meaning on a
warning sign without having to be able to read.

Here we have drawn **9** different **warning signs**.
For each sign, **choose** the correct **set of words** from the
shaded box and **write** those words in the **space** provided.

Pedestrian crossing No smoking Bikes not allowed	Radioactive material Speed limit 60 km/h Poison-not to be taken	Beach closed No swimming Kangaroos crossing
A _____ _____	B _____ _____	C _____ _____
D _____ _____	E _____ _____	F _____ _____
G _____ _____	H _____ _____	I _____ _____

3 - SENDING A MESSAGE

**What can you tell from the drawings
that you have just labelled on page 26?**
*Put a **tick beside** the **right** set of words
to **finish** each sentence.*

1 **The sign in box A warns that it is**
(a) too dangerous for swimming. ____
(b) too cold for swimming. ____

2 **The sign in box B means that**
(a) the contents are safe. ____
(b) the contents could poison you. ____

3 **The sign in box C means that cigarettes**
(a) can't be bought here. ____
(b) can't be smoked here. ____

4 **The sign in box D means that there is a**
(a) 60 kilometres per hour speed limit. ____
(b) roundabout 60 minutes away. ____

5 **The sign in box E means that**
(a) bicycles cannot be ridden. ____
(b) there are no bikes left for sale. ____

6 **The sign in box F warns swimmers**
(a) that the beach is closed. ____
(b) that there is surf carnival on. ____

7 **The sign in box G warns motorists that there**
(a) is a pedestrian crossing ahead. ____
(b) are pedestrians on the road. ____

8 **The sign in box H warns a motorists that**
(a) he has to wait for kangaroos. ____
(b) kangaroos might hop across the road. ____

9 **The sign in box I tells us that this area**
(a) has a radio station nearby. ____
(b) contains very dangerous material. ____

3 - SENDING A MESSAGE

Faces

The easiest way to send a message to someone in the **same room** as you, is with the **expression** on **your face**.

Here are drawings of the expressions on the faces
of **4 boys** and **5 girls**.
Choose a **word** from the **shaded box** that describes the
expression on each face.

| BOYS | - | Excited | Sad | Scared | Puzzled |
| GIRLS | - | Surprised | Angry | Sick | Tired | Happy |

A _ _ _ _ _ _ _ _ _ _

B _ _ _ _ _ _ _ _ _ _

C _ _ _ _ _ _ _ _ _ _

D _ _ _ _ _ _ _ _ _ _

E _ _ _ _ _ _ _ _ _ _

F _ _ _ _ _ _ _ _ _ _

G _ _ _ _ _ _ _ _ _ _

H _ _ _ _ _ _ _ _ _ _

I _ _ _ _ _ _ _ _ _ _

3 - SENDING A MESSAGE

What can you tell from the drawings that you have just labelled on page 28 ?

*Put a **tick** beside the right set of words to **finish** each sentence.*

1 **The girl in box A is**
(a) not wide awake. ____
(b) wide awake. ____

2 **The boy in box B looks**
(a) hungry. ____
(b) very frightened. ____

3 **The girl in box C**
(a) has a grin on her face. ____
(b) seems unwell. ____

4 **The boy in box D seems**
(a) to be worried about something. ____
(b) to be very sleepy. ____

5 **The girl in box E looks**
(a) quite calm. ____
(b) to be in a bad temper. ____

6 **The boy in box F is**
(a) not very happy. ____
(b) laughing. ____

7 **The girl in box G seems**
(a) pleased about something. ____
(b) very tired. ____

8 **The boy in box H**
(a) looks very worried. ____
(b) appears thrilled about something. ____

9 **The girl in box I seems**
(a) amazed by something. ____
(b) quite ill. ____

3 - SENDING A MESSAGE

Reading, writing, talking and **listening** are all ways
in which we **send** and **receive** messages.
They are forms of **communication**.

*Here we have drawn **9** different **forms of communication**.
Choose a **word** from the **shaded box** to **label** each one.*

Phone   Fax   Television   Radio   Newspaper
Comic   Book   Computer   Film

ROW 1

A _ _ _ _ _ _ _ _

B _ _ _ _ _ _ _ _

C _ _ _ _ _ _ _ _

ROW 2

D _ _ _ _ _ _ _ _

E _ _ _ _ _ _ _ _

F _ _ _ _ _ _ _ _

ROW 3

G _ _ _ _ _ _ _ _

H _ _ _ _ _ _ _ _

I _ _ _ _ _ _ _ _

CHAPTER 1 - ON THE MOVE

Page 3 - **A** Electric Tram   **B** Motor car   **C** Aeroplane
D Viking Ship   **E** Sailing Ship   **F** Steam Train

Page 4 - **Green** : car   train   bus   **Blue** : liner   sailing boat   launch
Yellow : plane   helicopter   **Red** : rocket

Page 5 - **1** (a)   **2** (b)   **3** (b)   **4** (a)   **5** (b)
6 No   **7** No   **8** Yes   **9** Yes   **10** Yes

Page 6 - **A** Petrol   **B** Papers   **C** Food   **D** Mail
E Soil   **F** Cement   **G** Cars

Page 7 - **1** (a)   **2** (b)   **3** (b)   **4** (a)   **5** (b)   **6** (b)
7 No   **8** Yes   **9** Yes

Page 8 - **A** Flying Doctor   **B** Ambulance   **C** Fire Engine
D Rescue Helicopter   **E** Police Car   **F** Surf Rescue

Page 9 - **1** (a)   **2** (a)   **3** (b)   **4** (a)   **5** (b)
6 Yes   **7** Yes   **8** No   **9** Yes   **10** Yes

Page 10 - **Purple** :   Glider   Sailing boat   Surf ski   Balloon
Red :   Surf boat   Aeroplane   Bus   Train
Orange :   Bike   Roller blades   Rowing boat

Page 11 - **1** (a)   **2** (b)   **3** (a)   **4** (a)   **5** (b)   **6** (b)   **7** (b)   **8** (b)

Page 12 - **Green** : **A** and **F**   **Yellow** : **B** and **H**
Blue : **C** and **E**   **Red** : **D** and **G**

Page 13 - **1** (a)   **2** (b)   **3** (b)   **4** (b)   **5** (b)   **6** (a)   **7** (a)   **8** (b)

Page 14 - **Land transport :** TRAIN   BUS   DRIVER   ROAD   RAIL   WHEELS
BIKE   CAR   TRUCK   STATION   TAXI.
Water transport : SEA   SAILOR   ROW   CANOE   FERRY   LINER
LAUNCH   WHARF   SAILS   OCEAN   TUG.
Air transport : BALLOON   SKY   SPACE   WINGS   GLIDER   ROCKET
PLANE   PILOT   FLYER   RUNWAY   AIRPORT

CHAPTER 2 - OUR WEATHER

Page 15 - **A** Wet   **B** Cold   **C** Sunny   **D** Windy   **E** Hot   **F** Cloudy

Page 16 - **1** (a) **Blue** : Second picture   (b) **Green** : First picture
2 A Snow   **B** Fog   **C** Hail   **D** Rain

Page 17 - **1** (b)   **2** (a)   **3** (a)   **4** (a)   **5** (a)
6 No   **7** No   **8** Yes   **9** Yes   **10** No

Page 18 -

Day A	Day B	Day C	Day D

Page 19 -   1 (a)   2 (b)   3 (b)   4 (a)   5 (b)   6 D   7 B   8 C   9 A   10 A

Page 20 -   **A** Grade 12   **B** Grade 10   **C** Grade 8
                 D Grade 6   **E** Grade 2

Page 21 -   1 (a)   2 (b)   3 (b)   4 (a)   5 (a)
               6 (b)   7 (b)   8 (b)

Page 22 -   **A** Spring   **B** Summer   **C** Autumn   **D** Winter

Page 23 -   1 (a)   2 (a)   3 (a)   4 (b)   5 (a)
               6 (a)   7 Summer   8 Winter   9 Autumn   10 Spring

Page 24 -   1 COLD   2 SUMMER   3 SPRING   4 WINDY   5 WINTER
               6 RAIN   7 AUTUMN   8 HOT   9 SEPTEMBER   10 STORM

CHAPTER 3 - SENDING A MESSAGE

Page 25 -   **Blue** : newspaper   comic   book
               Yellow : radio   television   telephone
               Red : no smoking   wheelchair   pedestrian crossing
               Green : the three faces

Page 26 -   **A** No swimming   **B** Poison - not to be taken   **C** No smoking
               D Speed limit 60 km/h   **E** Bikes not allowed   **F** Beach closed
               G Pedestrian crossing   **H** Kangaroos crossing   **I** Radioactive material

Page 27 -   1 (a)   2 (b)   3 (b)   4 (a)   5 (a)
               6 (a)   7 (a)   8 (b)   9 (b)

Page 28 -   **A** Tired   **B** Scared   **C** Sick   **D** Puzzled   **E** Angry
               F Sad   **G** Happy   **H** Excited   **I** Surprised

Page 29 -   1 (a)   2 (b)   3 (b)   4 (a)   5 (b)
               6 (a)   7 (a)   8 (b)   9 (a)

Page 30 -   **A** Phone   **B** Fax   **C** Computer   **D** Radio   **E** Film
               F Television   **G** Comic   **H** Newspaper   **I** Book

Page 31 -   1 (a)   2 (a)   3 (b)   4 (b)   5 (a)   6 (a)
               7 Row 3   8 Row 2   9 Row 1

Page 32 -   **A** - *Yellow*/girl - *Blue*/boy   **B** - *Yellow*/girl - *Blue*/Mum
 C - *Yellow*/girl   **D** - *Yellow*/boy - *Blue*/Dad

Page 33 -   **A** - The family waited outside for Grandpa.
 B - Dad put the beach gear in the boot.
 C - Jim sat on the back seat with Frisky.
 D - They found parking close to the beach.
 E - Frisky was safely tied to the umbrella.
 F - Mum decided it was time for lunch.

Page 34 -   **A** Runners   **B** Flags   **C** Smoke
 D Sticks   **E** Drums   **F** Pigeons

Page 35 -   **1** Flags   **2** Sticks   **3** Runners   **4** Pigeons   **5** Drums
 6 Smoke   **7** Yes   **8** Yes   **9** Yes

Page 36 -   **1** PURR   **2** BARK   **3** BRAY   **4** ROAR
 5 HISS   **6** SING   **7** MOOS   **8** CROW

CHAPTER 4 - LOOKING AROUND US

Page 37 -   **Blue** : dog kennel   teddy   lounge   stove   bed
 Yellow : blackboard   seat   school bag   lunch box   desk
 Green : crossroads   bus   police car   shop

Page 38 -   **A** Kitchen   **B** Family room   **C** Bathroom   **D** Bedroom

Page 39 -   **1** Bedroom   **2** Kitchen   **3** Bathroom   **4** Family room
 5 Kitchen   **6** Family room   **7** Bathroom   **8** Bedroom

Page 41 -   **1** (b)   **2** (a)   **3** (a)   **4** (b)   **5** (a)
 6 (b)   **7** (a)   **8** (a)   **9** (b)

Page 42 -   **A** Library   **B** Station   **C** Church
 D Shops   **E** Oval   **F** Park

Page 43 -   **1** (a)   **2** (b)   **3** (a)   **4** (b)   **5** (a)
 6 (a)   **7** No   **8** Yes   **9** Yes   **10** No

Page 44 -   **A** Country homestead   **B** Blocks of flats
 C Queensland house   **D** Suburban home

Page 45 -   **1** (b)   **2** (a)   **3** (a)   **4** (b)
 5 A block of flats   **6** A Queensland house
 7 A country homestead   **8** A suburban home

Page 46 -   **A** Crocodile   **B** Platypus   **C** Emu
 D Koala   **E** Kookaburra   **F** Kangaroo

Page 47 -   **1** Kookaburra   **2** Platypus   **3** Crocodile   **4** Koala   **5** Emu
 6 Kangaroo   **7** No   **8** No   **9** Yes   **10** (probably)

Page 48 -
1 GARDEN	2 WINTER	3 DRIVEWAY	4 LIGHTS
5 BATHROOM	6 BEDROOM	7 BLINDS	8 SUMMER
9 CARPETS	10 LAUNDRY	11 KITCHEN	

CHAPTER 5 - USING NATURE

Page 49 - **Brown** : hut boomerang cart canoe
Green : basket hat fishing net
Yellow : clothing weapon indian tent candles footwear
Orange : dish water carriers jug

Page 50 - **Green** : coffee table book bookcase table & chair tyre
carton newspaper boots.
Yellow : remaining 8 items.

Page 51 -
1 (a)	2 (b)	3 (a)	4 (b)	5 (b)
6 (a)	7 (a)	8 (b)		

Page 52 - **Blue** : jumper blanket socks   **Brown** : bag shoe belt
Green : doona pillow   **Yellow** : candles polish
Red : parachute scarf pyjamas

Page 53 -
1 (a)	2 (b)	3 (b)	4 (a)	5 (b)
6 (b)	7 (a)	8 (a)		

Page 54 - **Red** : pipe brick wall roof tiles brick pot pavers
Yellow : remaining 8 items.

Page 55 -
1 (b)	2 (a)	3 (b)	4 (a)	5 (b)
6 Yes	7 No	8 Yes	9 No	10 Yes

Page 56 - **Green** : book table & chair brick pot bag paper basket
bottle hat vase shoe candles wine glass
Yellow : remaining 9 items.

Page 57 -
1 plastic	2 leather	3 terracotta
4 nylon	5 glass	6 natural materials
7 natural materials		10 man-made materials

Page 58 - **Blue** : bottle glass vase
Green : flowers leaves peelings cut grass
Red : baby suit pyjamas skirts shirt
Yellow : carton comic newspaper box

Page 59 -
1 true	2 true	3 false	4 false
5 true	6 true	7 true	8 false
9 false	10 false		

Page 60 -
1 Sheets	2 Fibre	3 Trees	4 Bottles
5 Wool	6 Cattle	7 Feathers	8 Candles
9 Clay	10 Pearls	11 Roses	12 Colouring

3 - SENDING A MESSAGE

**What can you tell from the pictures and the
that you just labelled on page 30 ?**

*For exercises 1 to 6, put a **tick beside**
the **right** set of words to **finish** each of the sentences.*

1   **You would read the daily news**
    (a) in a newspaper.   ____
    (b) in a book.   ____

2   **Comics can have**
    (a) both pictures and stories.   ____
    (b) only pictures.   ____

3   **A radio gives you information**
    (a) using pictures.   ____
    (b) using sound.   ____

4   **To use a computer you have to**
    (a) be able to hear.   ____
    (b) use a keyboard.   ____

5   **Most family homes have**
    (a) a radio and a television set.   ____
    (b) a radio and a movie screen.   ____

6   **The easiest way to get in touch with a friend**
    (a) would be by radio.   ____
    (b) would be by phone.   ____

*For exercises 7 to 9, answer the following questions
with a **Row Number**.*

7   Which row contains three forms of
    written communication ?   ___

8   Which row contains three forms of
    communication that all use speech ?   ___

9   Which row contains three forms of
    communication that would be
    found in most offices ?   ___

3 - SENDING A MESSAGE

Talking and listening.
We can **send** messages by **talking**.
We can **receive** messages by **listening**.

From the **headings** given for each **picture**,
can you tell who is talking and who is listening ?
Use **yellow** to colour all the people that are **talking**.
Use **blue** to colour all the people that are **listening**.

A - "These are our holiday photos."

B - "I'm sorry, Mum, it was an accident !"

C - "My new dress has blue and red spots."

D - "I'm hungry. Is dinner ready yet, Dad ?"

3 - SENDING A MESSAGE

Reading and writing.

We can **receive** messages by **reading**.
We can **send** messages by **writing**.

*The best stories to **read** are those that have words and pictures. **Choose** the correct set of **words** from the **shaded boxes** and **write** them underneath each picture to **tell** the **story**.*

Mum decided it was time for lunch.	The family waited outside for Grandpa.	They found parking close to the beach.
Frisky was safely tied to the umbrella.	Dad put the beach gear in the boot.	Jim sat on the back seat with Frisky.

A _ _ _ _ _ _ _ _ _ _ _ _ _ _ _

B _ _ _ _ _ _ _ _ _ _ _ _ _ _ _

C _ _ _ _ _ _ _ _ _ _ _ _ _ _ _

D _ _ _ _ _ _ _ _ _ _ _ _ _ _ _

E _ _ _ _ _ _ _ _ _ _ _ _ _ _ _

F _ _ _ _ _ _ _ _ _ _ _ _ _ _ _

3 - SENDING A MESSAGE

Long ago, man had to rely on much **simpler means** than those we use today for sending messages.

We have shown **6 ways** messages were sent in **days gone by**. Use the **information** in the left-hand boxes to help you **label** each **picture**.

DRUMS
Native tribes could send messages with drum beats able to be heard over long distances.

PIGEONS
These birds have long been used to fly great distances carrying written messages from one place to another.

STICKS
Message sticks were used by Aborigines to deliver messages over long distances.

FLAGS
These were flown from ships' masts. This was the only way of sending a message from one warship to another.

SMOKE
Smoke signals were often used by Indian tribes to warn of the approach of enemies.

RUNNERS
In ancient times, people were given the job of running hundreds of kilometres to deliver messages during wars.

3 - SENDING A MESSAGE

What can you tell from the pictures and the information given on page 34 ?

*For exercises 1 to 6, choose **one** of your **headings** to answer each of the following questions.*

1   **Which method was used**
    to send a message from
    one warship to another ?   _____

2   **Which method was used**
    by Aborigines to send
    messages from tribe to tribe ?   _____

3   **Who were used**
    in ancient times to carry important
    messages during wars ?   _____

4   **What birds were used**
    to carry written messages
    over very long distances ?   _____

5   **What instruments were used**
    to beat out messages from
    one tribe to another ?   _____

6   **What part of a fire**
    sent signals between
    Indian tribes ?   _____

*For exercises 7 to 9, **write** either '**yes**' or '**no**'
to the following questions.*

7   Would you have to be able to **hear**
    to get a message from a drum ?   _____

8   Would you have to be able to **see**
    to understand the message from flags ?   _____

9   Would you have to be able to **read**
    to understand the message from a runner ?   _____

3 - SENDING A MESSAGE

Let's have fun with **coded** messages to end this topic.
Instead of using a **letter** we are going to use a
code for each letter.

A B C	D E F	G H I
J K L	M N O	P Q R
S T U	V W X	Y Z .

For example if we want to **write letter A**
we draw the sides of the box it is in.
Then we place a symbol ◆ in the **left hand** side of the box
(because A is in the left hand side)

like this ◆ ⌐

*This is all about the way **animals and birds communicate**.
The answers are all four-letter words.*
Crack the code and write your **answers** on the **lines given.**

1 Cats do this   _ _ _ _ _ _ _ _ _ _ _

2 Dogs do this   _ _ _ _ _ _ _ _ _ _ _

3 Donkeys do this   _ _ _ _ _ _ _ _ _ _ _

4 Lions do this   _ _ _ _ _ _ _ _ _ _ _

5 Snakes do this   _ _ _ _ _ _ _ _ _ _ _

6 Canaries do this   _ _ _ _ _ _ _ _ _ _ _

7 A cow does this   _ _ _ _ _ _ _ _ _ _ _

8 Roosters do this   _ _ _ _ _ _ _ _ _ _ _

CHAPTER 4 - LOOKING AROUND US

The things that are **around us**
are what make up our **environment**.

The things at **home** make up our **home environment**.
The things at **school** make up our **school environment**.
The things in our **local area** make up our **local environment**.

These pictures show things that you might find in
different types of environments.

*Use **blue** to colour things in your **home** environment*
*Use **yellow** to colour things in your **school** environment.*
*Use **green** to colour things in your **local** environment.*

4 - LOOKING AROUND US

A home environment.

Here we have drawn pictures showing
views of *4* different *rooms* in a *home environment*.

(a) Have fun **colouring** in each room.
(b) Choose a name from the shaded
     box to **label** each room.

Bedroom	Family Room	Kitchen	Bathroom

A _ _ _ _ _ _ _ _ _ _ _ _ _ _ _ _

B _ _ _ _ _ _ _ _ _ _ _ _ _ _ _ _

C _ _ _ _ _ _ _ _ _ _ _ _ _ _ _ _

D _ _ _ _ _ _ _ _ _ _ _ _ _ _ _ _

4 - LOOKING AROUND US

**What can you tell from the pictures
you just coloured and labelled on page 38 ?**

*Choose **one** of your **headings** to answer each
of the following questions.*

1   **Which of the rooms would you use**
to curl up in bed and read
a good book ?   _____

2   **Which room would your mother use**
to cook all the food
for a birthday party ?   _____

3   **Which room would your father use**
to shave and have a nice
warm bath ?   _____

4   **Which room would be used**
for sitting in front of the fire
and listening to music ?   _____

5   **Which room has**
a refrigerator, a sink
and flowers ?   _____

6   **Which room has**
a bookcase, a coffee table
and a cat ?   _____

7   **Which room has**
toilet paper, a duck
and two towel rails ?   _____

8   **Which room has**
pillows, a clock
and teddy bears ?   _____

4 - LOOKING AROUND US

Your school environment.

Below is a drawing of a typical **classroom environment**.
Now that you are school age, you spend a lot of your time
using the sorts of things shown in the drawing below.

***If you learn by correspondence, or are being home schooled,
you will use most of the things in this drawing.***

*1 - Have fun **colouring** this **picture**.*

*2 - Write a **short story** about the sort of **classroom** or
study you work in.*

----

4 - LOOKING AROUND US

**What can you tell from the picture
that you have just coloured in on page 40 ?**

*Put a **tick beside** the **right** set of words
to **finish** each sentence.*

1 **The globe of the world**
   (a) is hanging on the wall.   ____
   (b) is on the teacher's desk.   ____

2 **The teacher's name is**
   (a) Mrs Robins.   ____
   (b) Miss Robbins.   ____

3 **In the classroom there are**
   (a) 7 girls and 5 boys.   ____
   (b) 6 girls and 6 boys.   ____

4 **On the desks there is a total of**
   (a) 4 rulers and 2 pots of glue.   ____
   (b) 3 rulers and 2 pots of glue.   ____

5 **The alphabet chart is**
   (a) facing the windows.   ____
   (b) beside the windows.   ____

6 **There is a calendar on**
   (a) the back wall.   ____
   (b) the back of the door.   ____

7 **Every pupil in the room**
   (a) has an open book.   ____
   (b) has a pencil.   ____

8 **There are flowers**
   (a) on the teacher's desk.   ____
   (b) outside the window.   ____

9 **The answers to the sums on the board**
   (a) are 9 and 11.   ____
   (b) are 8 and 12.   ____

4 - LOOKING AROUND US

A local environment.

Here we have drawn **6 pictures** showing different parts
of a local environment.
Choose a **word** from the **shaded box** and **label** each **drawing**.

A _ _ _ _ _ _ _ _ _ _ _ _ _ _ _ _ _

B _ _ _ _ _ _ _ _ _ _ _ _ _ _ _ _ _

C _ _ _ _ _ _ _ _ _ _ _ _ _ _ _ _ _

D _ _ _ _ _ _ _ _ _ _ _ _ _ _ _ _ _

E _ _ _ _ _ _ _ _ _ _ _ _ _ _ _ _ _

F _ _ _ _ _ _ _ _ _ _ _ _ _ _ _ _ _

4 - LOOKING AROUND US

**What can you tell from the drawings
that you have just labelled on page 42 ?**

*For exercises 1 to 6, put a **tick beside**
the **right** set of words to **finish** each of the sentences.*

1   A library is where you go to
(a) borrow books.   ____
(b) buy books.   ____

2   The church is where people go to
(a) do their Sunday shopping.   ____
(b) attend Sunday service.   ____

3   The park would be a good place
(a) to play chasings.   ____
(b) to build sand castles. ____

4   The railway station is the place
(a) to catch planes.   ____
(b) to catch trains .   ____

5   One of the shops
(a) sells furniture.   ____
(b) sells plants.   ____

6   An oval is a special area for playing
(a) games like cricket and football.   ____
(b) games like tennis and golf.   ____

*For exercises 7 to 10, **write** either 'yes' or 'no'
to the following questions.*

7   Could you change a library book
       on Sunday ?   ----

8   Would you be able to take your dog
       for a walk in the park ?   ----

9   Are both the shops in the picture
       open ?   ----

10   Is the church clock showing
       5 o'clock ?   ----

4 - LOOKING AROUND US

Australia is a very **large country**.
Because it is so large, it has **many different environments.**

People have to live in all sorts of places **and all sorts of homes**.

Some people live in cities, some live in suburbs.   Some live out in the country and some live in the hot wet parts of northern Australia.

---

*We have **drawn 4 different** sorts of **Australian homes.***
*We have also given **description** of these homes.*

Read** the descriptions carefully and **choose** a **heading
for each picture.

Suburban home.	**Queensland house.**
The most popular type of home. It has its own front and back yard, often with room for a pool.	In the north of Australia many homes are raised up to allow cool air to flow underneath them.
Blocks of flats.	**Country homestead.**
Blocks of flats are also found in suburbs. They are usually quite close to rail or bus transport.	These are usually surrounded by lots of land and are often a long distance away from a town.

A _ _ _ _ _ _ _ _ _ _ _ _ _ _ _ _ _

B _ _ _ _ _ _ _ _ _ _ _ _ _ _ _ _ _

C _ _ _ _ _ _ _ _ _ _ _ _ _ _ _ _ _

D _ _ _ _ _ _ _ _ _ _ _ _ _ _ _ _ _

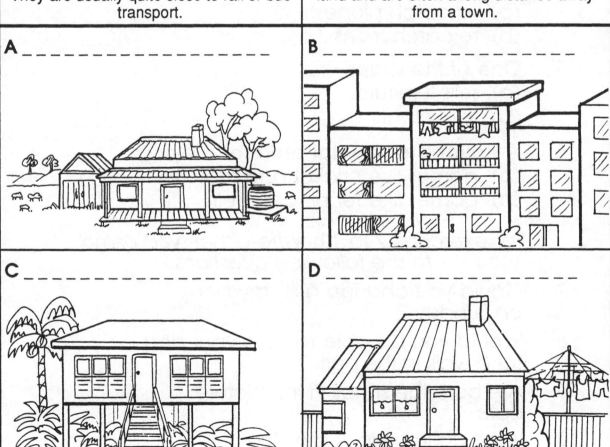

4 - LOOKING AROUND US

**What can you tell from the drawings
that you have just labelled on page 44 ?**

For exercises **1** *to* **4,** *put a* **tick beside**
the **right** *set of words to* **finish** *each of the sentences.*

1   A Queensland house
   (a) always has a swimming pool.   ____
   (b) is often raised to keep it cool.   ____

2   A country homestead
   (a) is usually surrounded by lots of land.   ____
   (b) is always close to a railway station.   ____

3   A suburban home
   (a) usually has a front and back garden.   ____
   (b) is kept cool with a swimming pool.   ____

4   A block of flats is usually
   (a) found out in the country.   ____
   (b) close to public transport.   ____

For exercises **5** *to* **8,** **answer** *each of the following
questions with the name of a* **type of home.**

Which home would you be likely to live in if

5   your family wanted a home close to public
   transport and with no lawns to mow ?

   _____

6   your family had to live in the hot northern states
   of Australia ?

   _____

7   your family raised sheep or cattle in the country
   areas of Australia ?

   _____

8   your father had a job in a city and your mother
   liked gardening ?

   _____

4 - LOOKING AROUND US

Australian animals and **plants** have their
own **environments** too !

Here we have drawn 6 different Australian environments.
How well do you know your Australian animals and birds ?
Choose a **name** from the **shaded box** to give each
drawing a **heading.**

Emu   Koala   Crocodile   Kookaburra   Platypus   Kangaroo

A _ _ _ _ _ _ _ _ _ _

B _ _ _ _ _ _ _ _ _ _

C _ _ _ _ _ _ _ _ _ _

D _ _ _ _ _ _ _ _ _ _

E _ _ _ _ _ _ _ _ _ _

F _ _ _ _ _ _ _ _ _ _

4 - LOOKING AROUND US

How much do you know about the Australian native creatures pictured on page 46 ?

For exercises 1 to 6, choose one of your headings to answer each of the following questions.

1   Which **bird** seems to be happy around people ?

_____

2   Which **animal** has webbed feet ?

_____

3   Which is Australia's most dangerous **reptile** ?

_____

4   Which **animal** lives on gum leaves ?

_____

5   What is the name of Australia's flightless **bird** ?

_____

6   Which **animal** carries its young in a pouch ?

_____

For exercises 7 to 10, write either 'yes' or 'no' to the following questions.

7   Do you think a platypus could live in the same river as a crocodile ?   ____

8   Do you think you would ever see an emu on your backyard fence ?   ____

9   Are gum leaves the only things koalas eat ?   ____

10   Have you ever heard a kookaburra laughing ?   ____

4 - LOOKING AROUND US

Here is a **WORD PUZZLE**.
How much have you learned about
home environments ?

						E					
1						E					
2						N					
3						V					
4						I					
5						R					
6						O					
7						N					
8						M					
9						E					
10						N					
11						T					

Fill in the missing words using the clues below.

1. The place where you might have flowers growing.
2. The season when you might have a heater on.
3. Cars use this to get from the street into a garage.
4. These are turned on at night so you can see.
5. The room where you clean your teeth.
6. The room where you sleep.
7. These are used on windows to keep out the sun.
8. The season when you might have a fan on.
9. These often cover floors in bedrooms.
10. The room where your mother washes the clothes.
11. The room where all the cooking takes place.

CHAPTER 5 - USING NATURE

Since earliest times, man has been using **nature**
to provide him with food, clothing and other things for
every day living.
Trees provided timber for shelters, carts and boats.
Plants provided straw and rope for hats, baskets and fishing nets.
Animal skins were used for clothing, tents and footwear.
Clay was used to make simple pottery dishes and jugs.

*Here we have some of the **earliest** things made from*
natural materials.
*Use **brown** to colour the things made from **trees**.*
*Use **green** to colour things made from **plant** materials.*
*Use **yellow** to colour things made from **animal** products.*
*Use **orange** to colour things made from **clay**.*

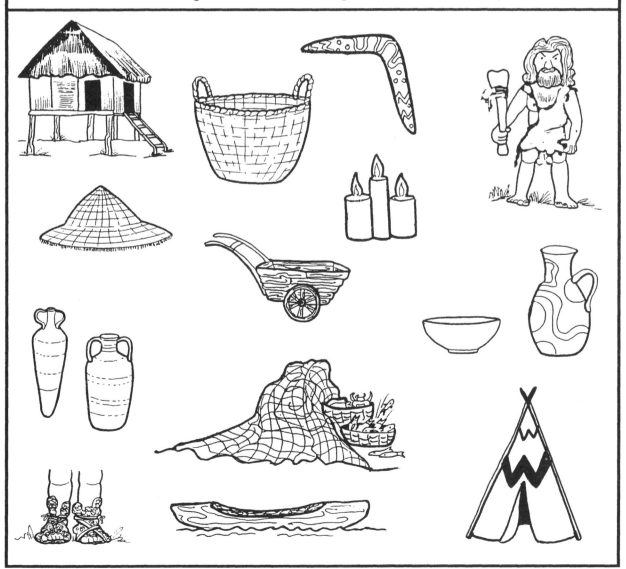

5 - USING NATURE

We still use **trees** and **plants** to provide us with things besides food.

With the help of **today's machines** we can make (*manufacture*) lots of goods from **trees** and **plants.**

Read the information in the boxes below then *colour* the drawings.
Use **green** for the things **manufactured** from **trees**.
Use **yellow** for the things **manufactured** from **plants**.

Linen and cotton threads, both come from **plants**. These threads are woven into cotton and linen fabric.	Sisal, hemp and raffia are tough **plant** fibres used to make mats, ropes, fishing nets and baskets.	The oils from many **plants** are used in perfumes, soaps and even some medicines.
Trees are cut and the timber is used to build houses and furniture.	Latex is collected from the rubber **tree** and made into rubber products like tyres.	Lots of paper and cardboard is made from the pulp of **trees**.

5 - USING NATURE

**What did you learn from the information given
and the pictures you just coloured in on page 50 ?**

*Put a **tick beside** the **right** set of words
to **finish** each sentence.*

1   A linen skirt would be made from
(a) plant fibre.   ____
(b) wood fibre.   ____

2   Car tyres are made from
(a) the fibres of the cotton plant.   ____
(b) rubber from a tree.   ____

3   Cardboard cartons are made from
(a) wood pulp.   ____
(b) tough raffia fibres.   ____

4   Paper is made from
(a) the paper plant.   ____
(b) wood pulp.   ____

5   Cotton pyjamas are made from
(a) the roots of the cotton tree.   ____
(b) material made from cotton fibre.   ____

6   Many clothes baskets are
(a) woven from raffia fibres.   ____
(b) woven from linen fibre.   ____

7   Perfume and soaps often have
(a) plant oils in them.   ____
(b) hemp fibres in them.   ____

8   To build a strong table
(a) you would use sisal.   ____
(b) you would use timber.   ____

5 - USING NATURE

We also use **animals** to provide us with things besides food.
Many things are made (*manufactured*) from
animal products.

Below we have a simple table showing some
goods made from **animal products**.

ANIMAL	PART USED	TURNED INTO	EXAMPLES
SHEEP	Fleece is shorn	Wool	Jumpers, socks, blankets.
CATTLE	Skins are tanned	Leather	Shoes, belts, handbags.
SILKWORMS	Cocoons are used	Silk	Parachutes, scarves, pyjamas
DUCKS	Birds are plucked	Feathers	Pillows, doonas.
BEES	Hives are stripped	Wax	Candles, polish.

Read the information above then colour the drawings as follows
*Use **blue** for **sheep** products. Use **brown** for **cattle** products.*
*Use **green** for **bird** products. Use **yellow** for **bee** products.*
*Use **red** to colour **silkworm** products.*

5 - USING NATURE

**What did you learn from the information given
and the pictures you just coloured in on page 52 ?**

*Put a **tick beside** the **right** set of words
to **finish** each sentence.*

1   **A woollen jumper would be made from**
    (a) the fleece of a sheep.   ____
    (b) the tanned hide of a cow.   ____

2   **A parachute would be made from**
    (a) material make from the silk plant.   ____
    (b) the fibres spun by a silkworm.   ____

3   **Leather handbags are made from**
    (a) the skin of sheep.   ____
    (b) the tanned hides of cattle.   ____

4   **Candles can be made from**
    (a) bees wax.   ____
    (b) grease from sheep's wool.   ____

5   **Doonas are made using**
    (a) sheep's wool.   ____
    (b) duck feathers.   ____

6   **Some furniture polish is made from**
    (a) silkworm cocoons.   ____
    (b) bees wax.   ____

7   **To knit some warm socks, mother might**
    (a) use wool.   ____
    (b) use leather.   ____

8   **To keep you warm in bed in winter**
    (a) you might have a feather doona.   ____
    (b) you would wear silk pyjamas.   ____

5 - USING NATURE

Clay and **sand** are two more things
that **nature provides** us with.
Clay is used to make **terracotta**.
Sand is used in the making of **glass**.

Read the information in the two boxes below.
*Use **red** to colour the things made from **terracotta**.*
*Use **yellow** to colour the things made from **glass**.*

TERRACOTTA

Terracotta is made from a mixture of clay and water. This mixture is formed into the shape wanted then it has to be baked. Very large hot ovens called **kilns** are used to **fire** the terracotta. Terracotta is very hard pottery used in making roof tiles, paving stones, garden pots and water pipes and bricks.

GLASS

Glass is just beach sand that is melted until it can be formed into the shape needed. To shape glass it is poured into a mould of the shape wanted. A blowpipe can also be used, the **molten** (melted) glass is blown into the right shape. Glass can also be decorated, or colours added while it is still molten. Many every day things are made of glass, probably one of the most important being windows and doors.

5 - USING NATURE

**What did you learn from the information given
and the pictures you just coloured in on page 54?**

*For exercises 1 to 5, put a **tick beside**
the **right** set of words to **finish** each of the sentences.*

1 **The tiles on the roof of a house would be**
   (a) made from a material using sand. ____
   (b) made from a material using clay. ____

2 **The windows in a house would be**
   (a) made from a material using sand. ____
   (b) made from a material using clay. ____

3 **Plants in the garden might be grown in pots**
   (a) made from glass. ____
   (b) made from terracotta. ____

4 **On your coffee table you might have**
   (a) a vase made from glass. ____
   (b) a vase made from bricks. ____

5 **The bricks of a house are probably**
   (a) made from melted sand. ____
   (b) made from terracotta. ____

*For exercises 6 to 10, **write** either **'yes' or 'no'**
to the following questions.*

6 Is it easy to break glass ? ____

7 Is it easy to break a brick ? ____

8 Can you see through glass ? ____

9 Can you see through terracotta ? ____

10 Can glass come in lots of colours ? ____

5 - USING NATURE

Of course **not all the things** that we use
are made of **natural** materials.

Things like plastic, vinyl, nylon, acrylic and polyester are used.
We call these man-made materials.

In order to **save** our **natural environments** we need
to **use** these **man-made items**
as well as things made from **natural materials.**

Colour the drawings below as follows.
*Use **green** for the things made from **natural materials.***
*Use **blue** for the things using **man-made** materials.*

5 - USING NATURE

**What did you learn from the pictures
you just coloured in on page 56?**

*For exercises 1 to 5, use **one** of the words printed in **bold**,
to complete each sentence. (Use each word **once** only).*

glass   plastic   nylon   terracotta   leather

1   The skateboard and the rubbish bin are made of

_____.

2   The shoe and the handbag are made of

_____.

3   The brick and the plant pot are made of

_____.

4.   The bicycle shorts and the bathers are made of

_____.

5   The wineglass and the bottle are made of

_____.

*For exercises 6 to 8, use **either one** of the following
sets of words to complete the sentences.*

man-made materials   natural materials

6   The table & chair set is made from

_____.

7   The candles and the hat are made from

_____.

8   The lunch box and gladwrap are made from

_____.

5 - USING NATURE

Re-cycling.

We have to make sure that **natural materials** are not **used up** more quickly than nature can provide them.

We have to conserve natural materials.
We can do this by re-cycling some of the things made from them.

Read the information below then colour the drawings as suggested.

Glass Re-cycling Bins	Compost Bins	Used Clothing Bins	Paper Re-cycling Bins
Glass can be collected and melted down, then used again to make bottles and jars.	All garden clippings, fruit & vegetable peelings and dead flowers can be collected in a compost bin and later used on the garden.	Clothes can be put into one of the many clothes bins that charities have available. Clothes that aren't passed along to other people are re-cycled into cleaning rags.	Paper products can be collected, turned back into pulp and then made into re-cycled paper.
Use **blue** to colour the things to go in here.	Use **green** to colour the things to go in here.	Use **red** to colour the things to go in here.	Use **yellow** to colour the things to go in here.

5 - USING NATURE

**What did you learn from the pictures
you just coloured in on page 58?**

*Write either **True** or **False** beside the following statements.*

1. Garden clippings are very good for
   making compost.   _ _ _ _ _ _ _

2. The skirts and the shirt could both
   be passed to someone in need.   _ _ _ _ _ _ _

3. Empty bottles and broken glass can
   be turned into pulp for paper.   _ _ _ _ _ _ _

4. Newspapers and magazines can
   be melted down for glass making.   _ _ _ _ _ _ _

5. The baby suit might be
   turned into cleaning rags.   _ _ _ _ _ _ _

6. Glass and paper bins are usually
   emptied by the garbage man.   _ _ _ _ _ _ _

7. Clothes bins are often located in
   shopping centre car parks.   _ _ _ _ _ _ _

8. Compost bins are usually kept on
   the footpath.   _ _ _ _ _ _ _

9. Glass and garden clippings can be
   put in the same bin.   _ _ _ _ _ _ _

10. Newspaper and old clothes can both
    be put in a clothes bin.   _ _ _ _ _ _ _

5 - USING NATURE

How much have you learned about Natural Materials ?

Fill in the **12 blank spaces** in the **TABLES** below
with a word from the **shaded boxes** underneath them.
The first **9** have been talked about in this chapter.
For the last 3 you might have to do some research.

	The Natural source	The Natural material	A product that is made
1	Cotton	Fabric	_____
2	Raffia	_____	Baskets
3	_____	Timber	Furniture
4	Sand	Glass	_____
5	Sheep	_____	Blankets
6	_____	Leather	Shoes
7	Ducks	_____	Pillows
8	Bees	Wax	_____
9	_____	Terracotta	Tiles
	Fibre	**Candles**	**Trees**
	Wool	**Bottles**	**Feathers**
	Sheets	**Cattle**	**Clay**
10	Oysters	_____	Necklaces
11	_____	Oil	Perfume
12	Beetles	Cochineal	_____
	Pearls	**Colouring**	**Roses**